Alfred's
**INSTRUMENTAL**
mp3 CD
**PLAY-ALONG**

# Ultimate
# Pop & Rock
## Instrumental Solos

**Arranged by Bill Galliford, Ethan Neuburg, and Tod Edmondson**
**Recordings produced by Dan Warner, Doug Emery, and Lee Levin.**

© 2012 Alfred Music Publishing Co., Inc.
All Rights Reserved. Printed in USA.

ISBN-10: 0-7390-9495-5
ISBN-13: 978-0-7390-9495-2

Alfred

**Alfred Cares.** Contents printed on 100% recycled paper.

# CONTENTS

| Song Title | Page | Demo | Track Play-Along |
|---|---|---|---|
| Tuning Note (A Concert) | | | 1 |
| 25 or 6 to 4 — Chicago | 3 | 2 | 3 |
| 21 Guns — Green Day | 4 | 4 | 5 |
| A Whiter Shade of Pale — Procol Harum | 6 | 6 | 7 |
| All I Have to Do Is Dream — The Everly Brothers | 8 | 8 | 9 |
| Animal — Neon Trees | 9 | 10 | 11 |
| Blueberry Hill — Fats Domino | 12 | 12 | 13 |
| Both Sides Now — Joni Mitchell | 13 | 14 | 15 |
| Boulevard of Broken Dreams — Green Day | 14 | 16 | 17 |
| Dancing Queen — Abba | 16 | 18 | 19 |
| Desperado — Eagles | 18 | 20 | 21 |
| Don't Stop Believin' — Journey | 20 | 22 | 23 |
| Domino — Jessie J | 22 | 24 | 25 |
| Dynamite — Taio Cruz | 24 | 26 | 27 |
| Everybody Talks — Neon Trees | 25 | 28 | 29 |
| Firework — Katy Perry | 28 | 30 | 31 |
| Forget You — Cee Lo Green | 30 | 32 | 33 |
| Gimme Some Lovin' — The Spencer Davis Group | 32 | 34 | 35 |
| Go Your Own Way — Fleetwood Mac | 33 | 36 | 37 |
| Good Time — Owl City and Carly Rae Jepsen | 34 | 38 | 39 |
| Grenade — Bruno Mars | 36 | 40 | 41 |
| (Your Love Keeps Lifting Me) Higher and Higher — Jackie Wilson | 38 | 42 | 43 |
| Home — Phillip Phillips | 40 | 44 | 45 |
| Honky Tonk Women — The Rolling Stones | 41 | 46 | 47 |
| Hotel California — Eagles | 42 | 48 | 49 |
| How Deep Is Your Love — Bee Gees | 45 | 50 | 51 |
| I Only Have Eyes for You — The Flamingos | 46 | 52 | 53 |
| In My Head — Jason Derülo | 47 | 54 | 55 |
| In the Midnight Hour — Wilson Pickett | 50 | 56 | 57 |
| Jar of Hearts — Christina Perri | 52 | 58 | 59 |
| Moondance — Van Morrison | 55 | 60 | 61 |
| Just A Kiss — Lady Antebellum | 56 | 62 | 63 |
| Just the Way You Are (Amazing) — Bruno Mars | 58 | 64 | 65 |
| Mr. Know It All — Kelly Clarkson | 60 | 66 | 67 |
| Need You Now — Lady Antebellum | 62 | 68 | 69 |
| Part of Me — Katy Perry | 64 | 70 | 71 |
| Payphone — Maroon 5 | 66 | 72 | 73 |
| (We're Gonna) Rock Around the Clock — Bill Haley and His Comets | 68 | 74 | 75 |
| (I Can't Get No) Satisfaction — The Rolling Stones | 69 | 76 | 77 |
| Rhythm of Love — Plain White T's | 70 | 78 | 79 |
| Smile — Uncle Kracker | 72 | 80 | 81 |
| Soul Man — Sam & Dave | 74 | 82 | 83 |
| Sunshine of Your Love — Cream | 75 | 84 | 85 |
| Spirit in the Sky — Norman Greenbaum | 76 | 86 | 87 |
| The Prayer — Celine Dion and Andrea Bocelli | 78 | 88 | 89 |
| We Are Young — fun. | 80 | 90 | 91 |
| When a Man Loves a Woman — Percy Sledge | 83 | 92 | 93 |
| Wide Awake — Katy Perry | 84 | 94 | 95 |
| You Raise Me Up — Josh Groban | 86 | 96 | 97 |
| You Send Me — Sam Cooke | 87 | 98 | 99 |

# 25 OR 6 TO 4

Words and Music by
ROBERT LAMM

Track 2: Demo
Track 3: Play-Along

**Moderately bright rock** (♩ = 144)

*molto rit.*

Track 4: Demo
Track 5: Play-Along

# 21 GUNS

Words and Music by
BILLIE JOE, GREEN DAY,
DAVID BOWIE and JOHN PHILLIPS

**Moderately slow** (♩ = 84)

21 Guns - 2 - 1

# A WHITER SHADE OF PALE

Track 6: Demo
Track 7: Play-Along

Words and Music by
KEITH REID and GARY BROOKER

A Whiter Shade of Pale - 2 - 1

# ALL I HAVE TO DO IS DREAM

Track 8: Demo
Track 9: Play-Along

Words and Music by
BOUDLEAUX BRYANT

Moderately (♩ = 104)

# ANIMAL

Words and Music by
TIM PAGNOTTA, TYLER GLENN,
BRANDEN CAMPBELL, ELAINE DOTY
and CHRISTOPHER ALLEN

Animal - 3 - 1

84 Chorus:

Track 12: Demo
Track 13: Play-Along

# BLUEBERRY HILL

Words and Music by
AL LEWIS, VINCENT ROSE
and LARRY STOCK

**Moderately slow (♩. = 92)**

Track 14: Demo
Track 15: Play-Along

# BOTH SIDES, NOW

Words and Music by
JONI MITCHELL

# BOULEVARD OF BROKEN DREAMS

Track 16: Demo
Track 17: Play-Along

Words by
BILLIE JOE

Music by
GREEN DAY

Boulevard of Broken Dreams - 2 - 1

Track 18: Demo
Track 19: Play-Along

# DANCING QUEEN

Words and Music by
BENNY ANDERSSON, STIG ANDERSON
and BJORN ULVAEUS

**Moderate disco beat** ♩ = 102

Dancing Queen - 2 - 1

Dancing Queen - 2 - 2

# DESPERADO

Track 20: Demo
Track 21: Play-Along

Words and Music by
DON HENLEY and GLENN FREY

Desperado - 2 - 1

Track 22: Demo
Track 23: Play-Along

# DON'T STOP BELIEVIN'

Words and Music by
JONATHAN CAIN, NEAL SCHON
and STEVE PERRY

**Moderate rock** (♩ = 120)

Don't Stop Believin' - 2 - 1

Don't Stop Believin' - 2 - 2

# DOMINO

Track 24: Demo
Track 25: Play-Along

Words and Music by
CLAUDE KELLY, LUKASZ GOTTWALD,
MAX MARTIN, HENRY WALTER
and JESSICA CORNISH

Moderate dance rock (♩ = 120)

Domino - 2 - 1

Track 26: Demo
Track 27: Play-Along

# DYNAMITE

Words and Music by
BONNIE McKEE, TAIO CRUZ,
LUKASZ GOTTWALD, MAX MARTIN
and BENJAMIN LEVIN

Moderate dance (♩ = 116)

Track 28: Demo
Track 29: Play-Along

# EVERYBODY TALKS

Words and Music by
TYLER GLENN and TIM PAGNOTTA

**Moderately fast rock (♩ = 152)**

Everybody Talks - 3 - 1

**48** 𝄋 *Chorus:*

*To Coda* ⊕

**62** *Bridge:*

**70**

*3*

1.

2.

Everybody Talks - 3 - 3

Along

# FIREWORK

Words and Music by
KATY PERRY, MIKKEL ERIKSEN,
TOR ERIK HERMANSEN, SANDY WILHELM
and ESTER DEAN

**Moderate rock** (♩ = 126)

Firework - 2 - 1

# FORGET YOU

Track 32: Demo
Track 33: Play-Along

Words and Music by
CHRISTOPHER BROWN, PETER HERNANDEZ,
ARI LEVINE, PHILIP LAWRENCE
and THOMAS CALLAWAY

Moderately bright soul (♩ = 126)

Forget You - 2 - 1

# GIMME SOME LOVIN'

Words and Music by
STEVE WINWOOD, MUFF WINWOOD
and SPENCER DAVIS

# GO YOUR OWN WAY

Words and Music by
LINDSEY BUCKINGHAM

Track 38: Demo
Track 39: Play-Along

# GOOD TIME

Words and Music by
MATTHEW THIESSEN, BRIAN LEE
and ADAM YOUNG

Moderate dance tempo (♩ = 120)

Good Time - 2 - 1

# GRENADE

Words and Music by
CLAUDE KELLY, PETER HERNANDEZ,
BRODY BROWN, PHILIP LAWRENCE,
ARI LEVINE and ANDREW WYATT

Grenade - 2 - 1

To Coda

36 Bridge:

D.S. ⅀ al Coda

Coda

# (YOUR LOVE KEEPS LIFTING ME) HIGHER AND HIGHER

Track 42: Demo
Track 43: Play-Along

Words and Music by
GARY JACKSON, CARL SMITH
and RAYNARD MINER

(Your Love Keeps Lifting Me) Higher and Higher - 2 - 1

(Your Love Keeps Lifting Me) Higher and Higher - 2 - 2

Track 44: Demo
Track 45: Play-Along

# HOME

Moderately (♩ = 120)

Words and Music by
DREW PEARSON and GREG HOLDEN

**Track 46: Demo**
**Track 47: Play-Along**

# HONKY TONK WOMEN

Words and Music by
MICK JAGGER and KEITH RICHARDS

**Moderate rock** (♩ = 116)

\* Percussion intro for accompaniment track.

# HOTEL CALIFORNIA

Words and Music by
DON HENLEY, GLENN FREY
and DON FELDER

Track 48: Demo
Track 49: Play-Along

Hotel California - 3 - 1

**25** %. *Chorus:*

**33** *Verse 2:*

*To Coda* ⊕

44

# HOW DEEP IS YOUR LOVE

Track 50: Demo
Track 51: Play-Along

Words and Music by
BARRY GIBB, MAURICE GIBB
and ROBIN GIBB

Track 52: Demo
Track 53: Play-Along

# I ONLY HAVE EYES FOR YOU

Words by
AL DUBIN

Music by
HARRY WARREN

Track 54: Demo
Track 55: Play-Along

# IN MY HEAD

Words and Music by
CLAUDE KELLY, JONATHAN ROTEM
and JASON DESROULEAUX

Moderate pop rock (♩ = 112)

In My Head - 3 - 1

In My Head - 3 - 3

# IN THE MIDNIGHT HOUR

Track 56: Demo
Track 57: Play-Along

Words by
**WILSON PICKETT**

Music by
**STEVE CROPPER**

In the Midnight Hour - 2 - 1

In the Midnight Hour - 2 - 2

Track 58: Demo
Track 59: Play-Along

# JAR OF HEARTS

Words and Music by
DREW LAWRENCE, CHRISTINA PERRI
and BARRETT YERETSIAN

Jar of Hearts - 3 - 1

# MOONDANCE

Track 60: Demo
Track 61: Play-Along

Words and Music by
VAN MORRISON

**Moderately fast jazz feel** (♩ = 132)

# JUST A KISS

Words and Music by
CHARLES KELLEY, DAVE HAYWOOD,
HILLARY SCOTT and DALLAS DAVIDSON

**Moderately slow (♩ = 72)**

Just a Kiss - 2 - 1

# JUST THE WAY YOU ARE (AMAZING)

Track 64: Demo
Track 65: Play-Along

Words and Music by
KHALIL WALTON, PETER HERNANDEZ,
PHILIP LAWRENCE, ARI LEVINE
and KHARI CAIN

**Moderately** (♩ = 112)

Just the Way You Are (Amazing) - 2 - 1

Just the Way You Are (Amazing) - 2 - 2

Track 66: Demo
Track 67: Play-Along

# MR. KNOW IT ALL

Words and Music by
**BRETT JAMES, ESTER DEAN,
BRIAN KENNEDY and DANTE JONES**

Moderate rock (♩ = 100)

Mr. Know It All - 2 - 1

Track 68: Demo
Track 69: Play-Along

# NEED YOU NOW

Words and Music by
DAVE HAYWOOD, CHARLES KELLEY,
HILLARY SCOTT and JOSH KEAR

**Moderately** (♩ = 108)

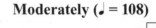

Need You Now - 2 - 1

Track 70: Demo
Track 71: Play-Along

# PART OF ME

Words and Music by
KATY PERRY, LUKASZ GOTTWALD,
MAX MARTIN and BONNIE McKEE

**Medium dance tempo (♩ = 132)**

Part of Me - 2 - 1

Track 72: Demo
Track 73: Play-Along

# PAYPHONE

Words and Music by
WIZ KHALIFA, ADAM LEVINE,
BENJAMIN LEVIN, AMMAR MALIK,
JOHAN SCHUSTER and DANIEL OMELIO

Payphone - 2 - 1

(WE'RE GONNA)
# ROCK AROUND THE CLOCK

Track 74: Demo
Track 75: Play-Along

Words and Music by
MAX C. FREEDMAN
and JIMMY DE KNIGHT

Moderately bright rock (♩ = 176)

# (I CAN'T GET NO) SATISFACTION

Track 76: Demo
Track 77: Play-Along

Words and Music by
MICK JAGGER and KEITH RICHARDS

Moderately, driving (♩ = 132)

Track 78: Demo
Track 79: Play-Along

# RHYTHM OF LOVE

Words and Music by
TIM LOPEZ

Rhythm of Love - 2 - 1

Track 80: Demo
Track 81: Play-Along

# SMILE

Words and Music by
MATTHEW SHAFER, BLAIR DALY,
J.T. HARDING and JEREMY BOSE

**Slow groove, half-time feel** (♩ = 72)

Smile - 2 - 1

Smile - 2 - 2

Track 82: Demo
Track 83: Play-Along

# SOUL MAN

Words and Music by
ISAAC HAYES and DAVID PORTER

Moderate R&B (♩ = 104)

# SUNSHINE OF YOUR LOVE

Track 84: Demo
Track 85: Play-Along

Words and Music by
JACK BRUCE, PETE BROWN
and ERIC CLAPTON

# SPIRIT IN THE SKY

Words and Music by
NORMAN GREENBAUM

Spirit in the Sky - 2 - 1

Spirit in the Sky - 2 - 2

# THE PRAYER

Track 88: Demo
Track 89: Play-Along

Words and Music by
CAROLE BAYER SAGER and DAVID FOSTER

The Prayer - 2 - 1

Track 90: Demo
Track 91: Play-Along

# WE ARE YOUNG

Words and Music by
NATE RUESS, ANDREW DOST,
JACK ANTONOFF and JEFFREY BHASKER

**Moderately (♩ = 120)**

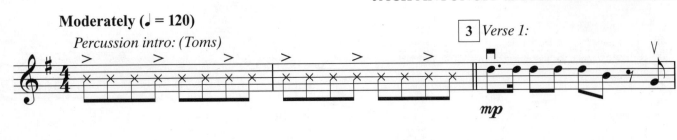

**19 Slower (♩ = 92)**

We Are Young - 3 - 1

# WHEN A MAN LOVES A WOMAN

Track 92: Demo
Track 93: Play-Along

Words and Music by
CALVIN LEWIS and ANDREW WRIGHT

Track 94: Demo
Track 95: Play-Along

# WIDE AWAKE

Words and Music by
KATY PERRY, BONNIE McKEE,
LUKASZ GOTTWALD, MAX MARTIN
and HENRY WALTER

Wide Awake - 2 - 1

# YOU RAISE ME UP

Track 96: Demo
Track 97: Play-Along

Words and Music by
ROLF LOVLAND and
BRENDAN GRAHAM

# YOU SEND ME

Track 98: Demo
Track 99: Play-Along

Words and Music by
SAM COOKE

# Harry Potter
# INSTRUMENTAL SOLOS

Play-along with the best-known themes from the Harry Potter film series! The compatible arrangements are carefully edited for the Level 2–3 player, and include an accompaniment CD which features a demo track and play-along track.

Titles: Double Trouble • Family Portrait • Farewell to Dobby • Fawkes the Phoenix • Fireworks • Harry in Winter • Harry's Wondrous World • Hedwig's Theme • Hogwarts' Hymn • Hogwarts' March • Leaving Hogwarts • Lily's Theme • Obliviate • Statues • A Window to the Past • Wizard Wheezes.

(00-39211) | Flute Book & CD | $12.99

(00-39214) | Clarinet Book & CD | $12.99

(00-39217) | Alto Sax Book & CD | $12.99

(00-39220) | Tenor Sax Book & CD | $12.99

(00-39223) | Trumpet Book & CD | $12.99

(00-39226) | Horn in F Book & CD | $12.99

(00-39229) | Trombone Book & CD | $12.99

(00-39232) | Piano Acc. Book & CD | $18.99

(00-39235) | Violin Book & CD | $18.99

(00-39238) | Viola Book & CD | $18.99

(00-39241) | Cello Book & CD | $18.99

Alto Saxophone · Level 2-3
SELECTIONS FROM THE
Harry Potter COMPLETE FILM SERIES
INSTRUMENTAL SOLOS